AF632667

Verses From My Tender Heart & Restless Mind

Amanda Tanui

BookLeaf Publishing

Verses From My Tender Heart & Restless Mind © 2022 Amanda Tanui

All rights reserved.

No part of this publication may be reproduced, stored in a retrieval system, or transmitted, in any form or by any means, electronic, mechanical, photocopying, recording or otherwise, without the prior written permission of the presenters.

Amanda Tanui asserts the moral right to be identified as author of this work.

Presentation by *BookLeaf Publishing*

Web: www.bookleafpub.com

E-mail: info@bookleafpub.com

ISBN : 9789357210867

First edition 2022

DEDICATION

To all who have encouraged my writing and believed in me even when I've not been so sure...you know who you are and I love you ❤

ACKNOWLEDGEMENT

Thank you to my 8th grade English teacher Mrs. Augustine, who has been a bright light in the life of many an awkward young teen, and who gave me a great bit of advice I've always held onto: to keep everything I write.

Special

Sometimes I wanna hate you
for doin' what you do -
for makin' me feel so bad,
but then makin' me feel so good.

Sometimes I wanna fix you;
wanna right the wrongs you've felt, wanna wrap
you in a warm embrace 'til the ice 'round your
frozen heart melts.

I don't think you're as bad as you seem,
but maybe that's just me being naive; feeling for
you much more than I should,
helplessly hoping it will turn out good.

I swore I'd never be a "someone to run to"
In my mind I believed that until I met you.
I never meant to care,
and tried hard not to fall,
but why should you settle for half a love
when we can have it all?

Neither of us is perfect
and we both know this is true,
but we bring each other sunshine

and make our lives less blue.

Perhaps I shouldn't tell you,
but I feel like you should know... you've become
so special to me
that I just can't let you go.

What If?

What if I never tell you?
What if you never know
that I have feelings for you,
and would like to let them grow...
into something more special
than any before,
If I knew you would share
and open the door
But then...

What if I pour my heart out to you?
What if you don't feel the same as I do?
Then I'll be left with nothing to say;
no hope in my heart for a happier day.
Would I still have a friend
I can always talk to?
Or would unreciprocated feelings
make me lose that too?

In Memory

Sometimes I think of something
  that I'd like to share with you
Something that would make you smile,
  maybe just a simple thought
Then I remember you're not here
  anymore
And your laughter in my memory is all
  that I've got.

For a tiny moment every now and
  then,
I think of stopping by -
Just to be in your company,
But then a tear comes to my eye…

You're not here anymore – you had to
  go
You needed relief – you were hurting
  so
God had mercy upon you,
  reaching down to take you home,
And as I look up into the heavens,
  I know that I'm never alone.

I feel your love like rays of sun

shining down onto my face.
I know from the warmth it radiates
that you're in a better place.
Although I'll never stop missing you
here with me, sharing all life's little
things,
I'll always be thankful to God who,
when you needed them, gave you
wings.

A Glimmer Of Hope

You, with your soulful brown eyes - so
deep and dark, while also bright
and playful
You, with your stories and ideas, and
refreshing childlike enthusiasm
You, who listens to my ramblings and
never tells me I'm wrong for my
feelings
You, who makes me laugh so much at
times, but also makes me think

You are so much more than some
people can see,
And I'm thankful that you share that
side of you with me.
I've never known anyone quite like
you, so genuine with such radiant
positivity
You are truly a bright part of my life -
you make me wanna believe...

Yes - YOU make me wanna believe
That "good things come to those who
wait"
Is not just something they say,

That it truly happens in its own time,
That "someday" could be today!
You make me wanna believe
That you could be sent from above;
I can't stop my heart from hoping -
You make me wanna believe...in love.

Intense

My body is restless tonight as I long
for your touch
My mind trips over thoughts of
missing you so much
I close my eyes and ache to feel your
lips on mine
A soft sigh escapes, hoping soon it
will be time

Just being in your presence brings a
calmness to my soul
Something I never expected,
something I can't control.
I feel safe with you to just be who I am
If no one understands, I don't give
a damn.

You're the fire that excites and
ignites me,
'Til I burn up and rise again...
I'm the cool water that covers and
calms you,
Flowing clear through your soul to
cleanse.

I Want

I want only to be with you
In a place all of our own
A place no one will find us
Where we can be alone

I want to feel your lips on mine
Your hands running through my hair
As we let our spirits intertwine
And you whisper that you care

I wanna feel your heartbeat against
  my skin,
As you trail hot kisses down my neck
I wanna hear my name breathlessly
As my hands play softly upon
  your back

I want only to be with you
And let our love flow free
Forget all things but me and you
And just make love to me

The Answer

What am I gonna do with you? you ask
And I can't find the words to answer;
Can't decide how to say it,
How to properly convey it.
I told you I'd show you, but you think
that I'm scared,
And maybe I am because I've never
dared
To put into words my desires for you -
All the sweet fantasies I hope will
come true...

Like when you accept my invitation
To a hot shower and some deviation
It all starts with a sweet little kiss
Igniting passion into intoxicating bliss
Sucking droplets of water from
tingling skin -
The wetter the better as the fun
begins
As you pull me closer in your arms
so strong,
I whisper that I've missed you, and
it's been so long.
Kisses growing deeper as our hands

explore
All the places on each other we've
been longing for
Lips pressing softly, tongues love
to mingle
Stirring fires within and everything
tingles

Off goes the water, and I lead you
to the bed
I've got desires to satisfy, cravings
to be fed
There, that's better - access to so
much more;
Bodies stretch longingly for mouths
to explore
Kisses and nibbles, sucking and licks
Orally fixated on getting our kicks
Juices are flowing - I'm so hot and wet
Reciprocal pleasure - we give what
we get
Breathing is ragged, hearts beating
fast;
A need for release yet desire to last

The world is gone - I've forgotten
it all
There's nothing but us and these
urges that call

And call me they do, and I let them
guide me
To quench these desires, I need you
inside me
Finally, at long last, our bodies
interlock
And sweetly grind together as
my hips start to rock;
Slow and sensual, then faster and
hard
I need you in the worst way - I've let
down my guard
No inhibitions, just a wet, wild ride
Passion builds hotter and hotter inside
Don't stop! Don't stop! It feels SO
right!
Bodies and souls explode together
In a million points of light!
Then, at last we lay together -
snuggled breast to chest;
You kiss me gently on my head - our
bodies are at rest.

Confession

I was sure if I wanted to do so
I could shut off my emotion,
And I thought that I had done it,
But now I shudder at such a notion.

I hoped that pretending not to care
Would make it reality,
So ever since you left me here,
I've denied that you matter to me.

The day we were over and done,
I knew it was better this way.
I stood in the shower for so long,
Trying to wash all your touches away.

I kept saying I wished I'd never
met you,
Even then knowing I'd never forget
you,
Cursing myself for being the fool to
let you
Do everything you did to me.

I never wanted to fall this way,

And I knew you couldn't be trusted.
Yet still I gave it all to you -
Everything for which you lusted.

I let your kisses convince me,
Your caresses and whispers
  persuaded;
Memories of them linger on my skin
Long after the love bites faded.

It's not fair that you remain in my heart
Long after you've left my arms
I was nothing to you, I guess
But another victim of your charms.

Still the thought stays with me
That I would turn back time
To bring back those moments
When I thought you were mine

I wanted you to love me,
I wanted "us" to work.
I hoped you were a good man,
And not just another jerk.

Some days I miss you so much
That I don't know what to do,
And although it makes no sense at all,
I really did love you.

Anxiety

FEAR
...of being lonely
...of not being loved
...of my feelings
AND UNCERTAINTY
...of you and me
...of the permanency of love
...have I given enough, or too much?
AND DOUBT
...that there'll be a happy ending
...that you really care
...that it's not all a lie
CLOSING IN
...is darkness
...is loneliness
...is coldness
AROUND ME
...is life and death
...are hopes and fears
...are smiles and tears
THAT WON'T LET ME
...be content
...keep hope alive
...feel secure

BE ME

So Now What?

So now what am I to do
As I sit alone, thinking
Wondering if you left because
you had to,
Or if you left because of me?

So now what happens
To all my dreams that were coming
true?
They can't live on memories
Of the love between me and you.

So now what do I do with this heart
That I felt break when we hugged
goodbye,
As the light inside gets dimmer
But the feelings there don't die?

So now what happens to these arms
That had gotten used to holding you?
They don't understand your absence;
They miss the warmth that they once
knew.

So now what is this body to do

That misses you so much?
So cold now is this smooth skin
That once burned beneath your touch.

So now what are these lips to do
That miss your tender kiss,
Unheard now whispering "I love you"
By all but the lonely winds?

So now what am I to do,
As I lie here wondering why,
Trying to keep the tears away
As my broken heart lies down to die?

Empty

Once a song had filled my heart
And joy flooded every hour
I gladly gave you everything
By my own willpower.

Once your presence filled my life
Every day was so brand new
My ears rang with the sound of
your voice
My heart sang melodies of you.

Now my life holds a vacant spot
That longs for your return
Sweet memories are all I've got,
And I know I'll never learn.

Now the song that filled my heart
Is a haunting melody
Of love that's gone, leaving me alone
My life, my heart - is empty.

You Never Know

When you look into these eyes
You never know what you'll see there
Traces of the tears they've cried
But you never know the hurt that's
truly there

When you say those words to me
You never know I don't believe
Just know that I won't say them back
Because I know someday you'll leave

You never know the love that burns
Inside this aching heart of mine
Love no one can ever have
Because it's trapped in time

You never know, each day
Just how much of me is left
Can I keep finding my way?
Will I have the strength?

You never know the loneliness here
That keeps me a prisoner still
You never know just how bad I feel -
Not now, and you never will.

Why Did God Choose You?

Of all the people that could've gone,
Why did God choose you?
You meant so much to everyone -
Your time ran out too soon.

I may not have said it, not even at
the end,
But you weren't just my grandpa -
You were my childhood playmate and
a friend.

The day I heard the dreadful news,
I burst into tears and ran to my room!
I never knew that morning when I'd
said goodbye,
I'd been saying it for the very last time

Now that it's too late, I know
If you love someone, you've gotta tell
them so
I wish I would've told you while you
were alive,
But where you are now, I know that
you realize

I'll always wish that you'd had more
time
I mean, what am I to do?
I don't understand the how's and
why's...
Why did God choose you?

A Dream

If you are only part of a dream
Then I want to stay asleep
Reality would hurt too much
'Cause my feelings run too deep.

If the warmth in your smile
Is just a beautiful thought
Then your image in my mind
Is the sweetest memory I've got.

Questions

Just knowing you brings me such joy
I want to tell you how I feel
But too many times my heart's been
a toy
Could this time be for real?

If I told you that I love you,
Would you turn on me?
Would you use my love to hurt me,
And then just leave me be?

If I looked into your eyes
And told you that I care
Would you say the same?
I need you to be there.

If I shared my dreams with you,
Would you tell me yours?
Could we make them all come true,
Or would you shut the door?

All these questions I need to ask
To know what you're about
I want to feel that I'll be loved
If I'm to pour my heart out

I need to know if in your arms
There'll be a place for me
To shelter my poor fragile heart
For only you to see

I need to know if you'll be there
With me until the end
To see me through and always care
As both a lover and a friend

Why Do I Love You?

Why do I love you, you ask
And why I do, I'm not sure
But then love is strange like that -
So elusive and mysterious, yet so pure

Maybe we try too hard to understand
Something that doesn't want to be
known
Perhaps we should just let love be,
And continue on as it has grown.

But apart from the enigma that is love,
I do know some things about us -
Something strong exists here
That neither you nor I can mistrust

I know that you were there for me
When I needed you most
When I felt my life was falling apart
When happiness and love became
ghosts
After all the hurt I've been through
When others left my heart for dead
You helped pick up the pieces -

You helped me love again

So why do I love you?
I hope now you can see
The reasons behind my feelings
Although love itself is a mystery

I love you because of who you are,
Although we don't always agree
Although you do have your faults too,
You still mean the world to me

You, To Me

You are always smiling, always
laughing - on the outside,
Making everyone around you smile
But what happens when those smiles
fade,
And the laughter is just an echo in
your mind?
Do you ever just come undone, fall
apart a little when you're all alone?

What emotions hide behind that smile
Or absorb into the darkness of those
laughing eyes?
If you always seem happy,
Who could ever think differently?
Who would ever suppose your smile
Is a mask for darker, unhappier
thoughts?

Perhaps someone who really listens
To not only what you say, but what
you don't say
Someone who wonders why you have
to be such a piece of work, such a
puzzle...

Someone who wonders what it is that
YOU want from life, and not what
you want the world to think...
Someone who's always been a captive
audient to your perplexity -
someone like me.

Kinda Tired

Kinda tired of falling for the wrong
guy all the time;
Kinda tired of giving up dreams of him
being mine.
Why can't it just work out for me?
Why is it never meant to be?
Being the bigger person who makes
the sacrifice -
Always bowing out, standing down,
always thinking twice...
And I'm kinda tired.

Kinda tired of being the loner 'cause
I can't have who I want,
But I won't half-ass it with just anyone,
will not put up a front.
Kinda tired of being questioned about
why I am alone,
While I wonder if I'll ever find the place
that is my home.
Yet despite my efforts to guard it, my
heart wants what it wants
And dives right in so recklessly - kinda
tired of its stunts

Your Kisses

I've been thinkin' 'bout your kisses -
They've been fondly on my mind,
In daydreams when a slow smile
lights my face,
Or as I lie down to sleep at night.
My eyelids flutter shut as I feel your
lips on mine
And a happy warm glow radiates my
being one more time

I can't describe what's special -
How a kiss can feel this way
I only know that I've felt it
Ever since the very first day

I don't remember every detail
Of the first time that we kissed,
But it's possible that angels sang -
I was filled with so much bliss!
Time stood still at that moment -
Everything else just faded.
New hope sprang into my heart
That had become so jaded.

Promises

If you give me your heart,
I'll treat it with care.
I'll give you mine too
So this love, we can share.

I'll shower you with affection,
And never leave your side.
I swear I'll always be there -
From you I'd never hide.

I'll be around to listen
To all your dreams and fears.
We'll help each other through
The sorrows and the tears.

I'll share in your laughter,
Delight in your smile -
With you in my life,
It's all so worthwhile.

I want you the way you are -
We should be together.
Don't change a thing -
Be your sweet self forever.

I Hope You Know

I hope you know how much you mean;
How important you are in my life
You've been such a breath of fresh air
Amidst all the struggles and strife

I hope you know just how much you're
loved
From the beginning and beyond the
end.
I never even knew I needed you,
But Heaven knew just who to send -
My little curly-haired angel
Who's saved me in so many ways
You've helped me see my purpose,
You've brought smiles to all my days.
I've made better choices because
of you,
Although things don't always go right.
You've made me want to reach higher
You've turned so much darkness to
light.

So I hope you never doubt that you
matter
Or feel you have nowhere to turn

I'm always here and I'll always care
And be empathetic to your concerns.
A mother's love is boundless;
I love you without measure
More precious than all else to me -
My sweet child I'll always treasure.

www.ingramcontent.com/pod-product-compliance
Lightning Source LLC
Chambersburg PA
CBHW051748130826
49812CB00033B/1048
9789357210867